THE DIVINE PLAN FOR JEW AND GENTILE

By

THE REV. PHILIP E. HUGHES, M.A., B.D.

I0834526

WIPF & STOCK · Eugene, Oregon

Wipf and Stock Publishers
199 W 8th Ave, Suite 3
Eugene, OR 97401

The Divine Plan for Jew and Gentile
By Hughes, Philip E.
Copyright©1949 Inter-Varsity Press, UK
ISBN 13: 978-1-60899-470-0
Publication date 2/15/2010
Previously published by The Tyndale Press, 1949

This limited edition licensed by special permission of Inter-Varsity Press, UK.

THE DIVINE PLAN FOR JEW AND GENTILE

THE place of the Jew in the purposes of God is not only a subject of increasing importance and significance in our world today, but one which calls for a diligent searching of the Scriptures and a reverent application of the principles of interpretation as set forth in the New Testament. In the following pages I shall endeavour to indicate the chief lines of the Biblical teaching on this subject, using St. Paul's well-known parable of the olive tree in Romans xi as a framework upon which to stretch the canvas depicting God's purposes as they affect both Jews and Gentiles.

I. THE ROOT OF THE TREE

The root of the Apostle's olive tree is grounded in the subsoil of the protevangelium of Genesis iii. 15. Here we have the earliest gospel promise, proclaimed to the fallen parents of the human race. In them we find human nature brought into a state of sin and condemnation, and in desperate need of superhuman help. And in this promise the grace and mercy of Almighty God are manifested from the very first moment of man's dire need; for, so far from descending upon His guilty creatures in the mere office of a wrathful and implacable Judge, God committed to them a prophecy in which was enshrined the hope that the divine-human communion might be restored. Even before pronouncing sentence upon their sin, He entrusted to them the merciful promise of a great Deliverer and the certain hope of ultimate victory over the fearsome enemy of their souls.

The serpent was to bruise the Saviour's heel: this, as we now know, was fulfilled when Christ suffered and died upon the cross of Calvary. But it was a wound from which the Saviour was to recover; Satan could touch only His heel, the lowest part of our Lord, that is, His humanity: His Deity is inviolable. The Saviour, however, was to crush the serpent's head; whereby it was foreshadowed that Satan would receive a wound unto death. The resurrection of our Lord from the dead has set the seal upon His supremacy and established Him as the assured Overcomer in the great struggle against the forces of evil.

But this promise was necessarily of a general and shadowy nature: it was a mysterious adumbration of the outcome of the conflict with Satan, and at the same time a gracious assurance to man that God had not entirely cast him away nor disassociated Himself from the welfare of His erring creatures. It was a message of hope to the whole human race. But the particularities of its fulfilment remained to be unfolded in later ages.

Now we pass on to God's covenant with the patriarch Abraham, for this is the very tap-root of the Pauline olive tree. The obedience and faith of the patriarch were acceptable to God and called forth the remarkable promise to the effect that he, although at the time aged and childless, would become 'exceeding fruitful,' the father of nations and kings; that his seed would be multiplied until it became a 'great nation,' in number 'as the stars of the heaven, and as the sand which is upon the sea shore'; that the land of Canaan, wherein he was a stranger, would be given to him and to his posterity for an everlasting possession; and that he would both be blessed and also become a blessing —indeed, that in him and in his seed should 'all the families of the earth be blessed' (Gn. xii. 2, 3, xiii. 16, xv. 5, 18, xvii. 2, 6-8, xviii. 18, xxii. 17, 18).

In attempting to interpret these notable predictions, it is important for us to bear in mind that they carry a double connotation: on the one hand, they are to be understood in a material or outward sense, and, on the other, in a spiritual or inner sense. The study of Scripture itself teaches us (as I shall hope to prove) to distinguish between what we may call their proximate and their ultimate signification.

In the first place, then, let us consider in what manner these prophecies given by God to Abraham have been outwardly fulfilled. The prediction that from him would spring a great nation, and that his posterity would be multiplied as the stars of the heaven and as the sand of the sea shore, has found its material fulfilment, not merely in the vast numbers of those peoples which in later times could justly trace back their lineage to Abraham as their forebear, but more particularly in the Israelitish nation whose amazing prolificity was one of the outstanding characteristics of their sojourn in Egypt: 'The children of Israel were fruitful, and increased abundantly, and multiplied, and waxed exceeding mighty; and the land was filled with them' (Ex. i. 7). This was doubly remarkable, inasmuch as the little family band of seventy or so persons who originally formed a settlement in the district of Goshen were not, as might have been expected (especially as their close kinsman Joseph was, under Pharaoh, the first man of the land), assimilated into what was then the far greater body of the Egyptians. Throughout the whole length of their sojourn in this country, a period of more than two hundred years, they maintained their identity intact and their blood unmixed. In this manner God was preparing them to become the 'great nation' whom He would choose for the setting forward of His purposes of blessing to the whole world.

The hand of God was in all this, and Moses reminded the Israelites of this patent truth when, at the conclusion of their forty years of wandering in the wilderness, he addressed them in the following terms: 'Thy fathers went down into Egypt with threescore and ten persons; and now the Lord thy God hath made thee as the stars of heaven for multitude' (Dt. x. 22; cf. i. 10). Words such as these make it evident that Moses was satisfied that God had indeed *literally* fulfilled this aspect of the promise made to

Abraham. Moreover, that great leader and lawgiver, who was not permitted to pass over Jordan into Canaan with the people of Israel, enjoined upon them that, when once they were possessors of the promised land and in due course brought their offering of first-fruits to the priest, they were to acknowledge before the Lord their God and say: 'A Syrian ready to perish was my father, and he went down into Egypt, and sojourned there, few in number; and he became there a nation, great, mighty, and populous' (Dt. xxvi. 5).

The rhetorical question of Balaam, the Mesopotamian prophet, also bears testimony to the marvellous development of the children of Israel into a numerous people: 'Who can count the dust of Jacob, or number the fourth part of Israel?' (Nu. xxiii. 10). Solomon, too, in a subsequent age, was impressed by this same phenomenon: 'Thy servant is in the midst of thy people which thou hast chosen, a great people, that cannot be numbered nor counted for multitude' (I Ki. iii. 8).

In like manner we may observe how the promise that the land of Canaan would be given to Abraham's seed was performed to the letter. At the termination of the forty years in the wilderness the Israelites crossed over the river Jordan under the leadership of Joshua, and proceeded to make conquest of the land of Canaan. Here they dwelt for more than seven hundred years (the southern tribes for more than eight hundred years) until their apostasy caused them to be carried off into ignominious captivity in heathen lands. Those that subsequently returned, and their descendants after them, established themselves once more in Palestine, and remained as the people of the land for a further period of six hundred years, until the overthrow of Jerusalem by the Romans. In dedicating the first-fruits of the earth to the Lord, the Israelite had been commanded to say, 'I profess this day that I am come into the country which the Lord sware unto our fathers for to give us' (Dt. xxvi. 3), thus acknowledging the faithfulness of God in the keeping of this aspect also of the promise made to Abraham many generations previously. And this fulfilment of the divine word is further confirmed by the writer of the book of Joshua with these clinching sentences: 'And the Lord gave unto Israel all the land which He sware to give unto their fathers; and they possessed it, and dwelt therein. And the Lord gave them rest round about, according to all that He sware unto their fathers: and there stood not a man of all their enemies before them; the Lord delivered all their enemies into their hand. There failed not aught of any good thing which the Lord had spoken unto the house of Israel; *all came to pass*' (Jos. xxi. 43-45).

Furthermore, in making His covenant with Abraham, God had actually indicated the bounds of the promised land as being 'from the river of Egypt unto the great river, the river Euphrates' (Gn. xv. 18). These delimitations were repeated to Moses: 'I will set thy border from the Red Sea even unto the sea of the Philistines, and from the wilderness unto the river,' that is, the river Euphrates; and they were confirmed in turn to his successor Joshua (Ex. xxiii. 31; Jos. i. 4). But at the same time the Israelites were forewarned not to expect to occupy all this territory in its entirety as soon as they entered into the land; the conquest of their enemies was to be a gradual one, and the reason given was one of great ecological soundness and foresight: 'I will not drive them out from before thee in one year, lest the land become desolate, and the beast of the field multiply against thee. By little and little I will drive them out from before thee, until thou be increased, and inherit the land' (Ex. xxiii. 29, 30). It was not until the reign of Solomon, some five hundred years later, that these conditions were finally realized. In those days, we are told, 'Judah and Israel were many, as the sand which is by the sea in multitude, eating, and drinking, and making merry. And Solomon ruled over all the kingdom from the river unto the land of the Philistines, and unto the border of Egypt. . . . He had dominion over all the region on this side of the river, from Tiphsah even to Gaza, over all the kings on this side of the river: and he had peace on all sides round about him. And Judah and Israel dwelt safely, every man under his vine and under his fig tree, from Dan even to Beer-Sheba, all the days of Solomon' (1 Ki. iv. 20-25).

Psalm cv, that great hymn of praise and gratitude to God, celebrates expressly the perfect faithfulness of Jehovah by acknowledging the remarkable manner in which He had performed His solemn covenant made with Abraham. The whole Psalm is relevant and is parallel with David's hymn in 1 Chronicles xvi. 7-36. The import of statements such as those which, for the sake of brevity, I now select, can scarcely be mistaken: 'He hath remembered His covenant for ever, the word which He commanded to a thousand generations; which covenant He made with Abraham, and His oath unto Isaac, . . . He remembered His holy promise, and Abraham His servant. And He brought forth His people with joy, and His chosen with gladness: and gave them the lands of the heathen: and they inherited the labour of the people; that they might observe His statutes, and keep His laws. Praise ye the Lord!' (Ps. cv. 8, 9, 42-45).

Four hundred years after the reign of Solomon, the Levites who returned from the Babylonian captivity with Nehemiah publicly made a solemn confession and acknowledgment before God, from which I take the following significant statements: 'Thou art the Lord the God, who didst choose Abram, and broughtest him forth out of Ur of the Chaldees, and gavest him the name of Abraham; and foundest his heart faithful before Thee, and madest a covenant with him to give him the land of the Canaanites, the Hittites, the Amorites, and the Perrizites, and the Jebusites, and the Girgashites, even to give it unto his seed, *and hast performed Thy words;* for Thou art righteous: and didst see the affliction of our fathers in Egypt, and heardest their cry by the Red Sea. . . . Their children also multipliedst thou as the stars of heaven, and broughtest them into the land, concerning which thou didst say to their fathers, that they should go in to possess it. So the children went in and possessed the land, . . . and delighted themselves in Thy great goodness' (Ne. ix. 7-9, 23-25).

And so we see how the promises to Abraham of old were, in their externals at least, quite definitely fulfilled, how his seed became a great nation and inherited the promised land in accordance with the limits which God had foretold. Nor is this a mere personal conclusion, but one (as I have shown) that is attested in the plainest possible terms by Holy Scripture itself. By disregarding this testimony many excellent persons have arrived at incorrect conclusions concerning the future of Palestine and the Jews.

II. THE FATNESS OF THE TREE

But, it will be objected, this land was promised not only to Abraham's posterity, but even to the patriarch himself, as an '*everlasting* possession,' and it is certainly known that Abraham was a stranger in Canaan until the day of his death, and that his posterity have not enjoyed the possession of it uninterruptedly: how, then, can it be true that God's word has been performed? To this it must be replied that it is just here, in connection with this very point, that we begin to be brought face to face with the ultimate or spiritual meaning of the Abrahamic covenant.

When God said to Abraham, 'I will give unto thee, and to thy seed after thee, the land wherein thou art a stranger, for an everlasting possession,' what exactly did He mean? Did God promise the patriarch merely an earthly acquisition? If so, subsequent events have clearly shown that the promise has not been kept. It cannot be disputed that the country of Canaan has not been an everlasting possession either of Abraham or of his seed: at best, they have only enjoyed a footing in this land at intermittent intervals; and for a period of approximately eighteen hundred years since the final anti-Roman revolt under Bar-Cochba this territory has been the possession of Gentile peoples, and in no sense of the seed of Abraham through Isaac. Yet we dare not charge Almighty God with unfaithfulness or, alternatively, with inability to perform what He had promised.

There is beyond doubt much truth in the contention that, just as the covenant with Abraham was made in consequence of his faith and obedience, so, too, the continuance of that covenant presupposed the condition of faith and obedience in his posterity: an unfaithful and disobedient people could not expect to partake of the blessings and benefits of the covenant. Moses, in fact, warned the children of Israel to this very effect: 'Take heed unto yourselves, lest ye forget the covenant of the Lord your God, which He made with you. . . . I call heaven and earth to witness against you this day, that ye shall soon utterly perish from off the land whereunto ye go over Jordan to possess it: ye shall not prolong your days upon it, but shall utterly be destroyed; and the Lord shall scatter you among the peoples, and ye shall be left few in number among the nations' (Dt. iv. 23-27). It was with words of similar import that God admonished Solomon to the effect that if the people forsook His statutes and served other gods, then they would be plucked up by the roots out of the land which they had been given, and the temple which He had sanctified would be cast out of His sight and made a proverb and a byword among all nations. To the astonished passer-by who should inquire, 'Why hath the Lord done thus unto this land and unto this house?' it would be answered, 'Because they forsook the Lord God of their fathers, which brought them forth out of the land of Egypt, and laid hold on other gods, and worshipped them, and served them: therefore hath He brought all this evil upon them' (see 2 Ch. vii. 19-22).

Subsequent history has provided the clearest possible practical demonstration that the apostasy of the Jewish nation has caused them to forfeit, through their own folly, the divine favour and blessing. This is a terrible example to all other nations, the British included, of the bitter and inevitable consequence of self-righteousness and unfaithfulness to God, and of the abuse of a position of privilege.

Those Jews who returned from Babylonian captivity to Jerusalem, after experiencing the stern judgment of God upon their disobedience, were under no illusions concerning the guilt of their nation, but solemnly acknowledged the justice of their punishment: 'Howbeit Thou art just in all that is come upon us; for Thou hast dealt truly, but we have done wickedly' (Ne. ix. 33, R.V.).

Yet these considerations do not greatly assist us in the present difficulty, for it is not elsewhere God's custom to fix His creatures' attention upon earthly prospects, but rather to cause them to look away from this transitory world to the eternal values of the heavenly reality. Let us not forget either that the whole world labours and groans under the curse which followed upon man's sin (Rom. viii. 22); it is hard to believe that God would promise for eternity something upon which a curse already rested, something indeed which, even under the happiest of circumstances, could be enjoyed by each individual only for the brief and fleeting term of his life's span upon this earth; and a territory, moreover, which, should there be, as some have fondly imagined, an assemblage on some future resurrection day of all the generations that are descended along the line of promise from Abraham, would be altogether inadequate for the accommodation of so vast a multitude.

Surely, if they learnt anything, the patriarchs learnt to mistrust any object of this world for the satisfaction of their deepest cravings. Abraham's obedience to the call of God conducted him to a life of rigour and vicissitude and temporal uncertainty, and to the endurance of climatic extremes with no better shelter than the flimsy covering of a tent—an existence in sharp contrast to his secure mode of life in the great city of Ur. As Calvin reminds us in a fine passage (*Inst.* II. x. 11), 'he is torn away from friends, parents, and country, objects in which the chief happiness of life is deemed to consist, as if it had been the fixed purpose of God to deprive him of all the sources of enjoyment.

No sooner does he enter into the land in which he was ordered to dwell, than he is driven from it by famine. In the country to which he retires to obtain relief, he is obliged, for his personal safety, to expose his wife to prostitution. This must have been more bitter than many deaths. After returning to the land of his habitation, he is again expelled by famine. What is the happiness of inhabiting a land where you must often suffer from hunger, nay perish from famine, unless you flee from it? . . . He wanders up and down uncertain for many years. . . . Wherever he goes he meets with savage-hearted neighbours, who will not even allow him to drink of the wells which he has dug with great labour. . . . Thus, in fine, during the whole course of his life, he was harassed and tossed in such a way, that anyone desirous of giving a picture of a calamitous life could not find one more appropriate.'

Although at a later time the descendants of Abraham inhabited the land of Canaan with more or less security for a period of some centuries, we must not forget that the territory was promised not only to the seed of Abraham, but to Abraham himself also, who was an unsettled stranger there, 'for an everlasting possession' (Gn. xvii. 8). But this world, and all that is in it, is transitory. Such happiness as is to be found here is ephemeral, and the enjoyment of it but partial; and man's earthly course is brief and torn with yearnings after a better state (cf. 1 Jn. ii. 15-17). Are we then to charge God with the use of contradictory terms when He promises an earthly territory as 'an everlasting possession'? Was the Almighty indeed leading the patriarch to indulge in the vain hope of possessing for eternity that which must ultimately in the nature of things perish?

By no means. We do not think of accusing Christ of inconsistency or insincerity when the Scripture tells us that, His body and blood intact before them, He gave His disciples bread and wine with the words, 'This is My body,' and 'This is My blood.' Had He intended these statements literally, He would literally have given them of His own actual flesh and blood, and the very fact that He did not do so, but, while He Himself was bodily present with them, handed them the humble symbols of bread and wine to the accompaniment of these remarkable words, indicates that these words were intended in anything but a carnal sense, that they were, in fact, intended in a spiritual sense. The visible elements of bread and wine were not intended simply as a source of sustenance for the bodily frame, but rather as a tangible token of the invisible and spiritual power which sustains the life of the soul that is united to Christ and feeds upon Him by faith. We do not come to the Holy Communion for a physical meal, but that our hearts and thoughts may be transported to heaven, whither our Saviour is gone before us. No more did Abraham and the other patriarchs seek in the visible land of Canaan their everlasting possession, nor interpret in a carnal manner the good things promised by God. Had they done so, they would have been bitterly disillusioned men. But they looked beyond to the enjoyment of an eternal state which, though hidden from the physical gaze, was none the less apparent to the eye of faith.

The truth is that the promise to Abraham of an 'everlasting' possession and the strong contrast opposed by the ills and hardships of his earthly existence were intended to direct his aspirations away from the idea of gaining any corruptible inheritance, and up into the very presence of the eternal God, where there is 'fulness of joy,' and at whose right hand there are 'pleasures for evermore' (Ps. xvi. 11). This, in fact, was the significance of God's word to the patriarch: 'Fear not, Abram; I am thy shield, and thy exceeding great reward' (Gn. xv. 1). His exceeding great reward was to be sought and found in the eternal God, and not in any merely mundane acquisition. Thus he got the true perspective of the man of faith.

Had it been the case that Abraham's hopes were centred chiefly in the securing of an earthly possession, upon entering the promised land, he would doubtless have attempted to exchange the fragile abode afforded by his tents for a more solid and permanent type of dwelling place. But the very fact that he continued to dwell in tents is set before us as a clear indication that 'he looked for a city which hath foundations, whose builder and maker is God' (Heb. xi. 9, 10). The early patriarchs—Abel who was murdered by the hand of his own brother, Enoch whose earnest preaching of coming judgment fell upon the unreceptive ears of the ungodly people of his day (Jude 14, 15), Noah who by the providence of God survived what is probably the most terrifying ordeal ever experienced by man, and Abraham at whose precarious existence we have already glanced—all these, by their constant faith in the midst of the most harassing adversities, 'confessed that they were strangers and pilgrims on the earth,' and declared 'plainly that they were seeking a country.' What sort of a country? An earthly one? No! For had this been their quest they might quite well, as the apostolic writer suggests, have returned to 'that country from whence they came out.' But no: they desired '*a better country, that is, a heavenly:* wherefore God is not ashamed of them, to be called their God; for He hath prepared for them a city' (Heb. xi. 13-16). Consequently, the same author reminds us that, like these faithful men of old, '*here we have no continuing city, but we seek one to come*' (Heb. xiii. 14).

The observations just made demonstrate with great clarity that Abraham's expectation was by no means focused upon that which is immediately perceptible to the physical senses, but rather that the country he sought was one not of this earth. Calvin remarks that, if the 'holy patriarchs expected a happy life from the hand of God (and it is indubitable that they did), they viewed and contemplated a different happiness from that of a terrestrial life' (*Inst.* II. x. 13). Together with the patriarchs and St. Paul and all thoroughgoing Christians of every age, we have to learn the great and vital lessons that 'our citizenship is in heaven,' not on this earth (Phil. iii. 20); that the earthly Jerusalem, 'Jerusalem which now is, is in bondage with her children, but *Jerusalem which is above is free,* which is the mother of us all'; that in very truth they and we 'are not children of the bondwoman, but of the free' (Gal. iv. 22-31).

Hence the force of the Pauline injunction to '*seek those things which are above,* where Christ sitteth on the right hand of God.' '*Set your affections on things above,*' he urges, '*not on things on the earth*' (Col. iii. 1, 2).

The conclusions of that great Apostle, whose obedience to the call of Christ led him to a life of suffering beyond even the measure of that endured by Abraham, are entirely applicable to the lives of the patriarchs of old: 'For I reckon,' says that saintly man, 'that the sufferings of this present time are not worthy to be compared with the glory that shall be revealed in us. . . . Wherefore we faint not; but though our outward man is decaying, yet our inward man is renewed day by day. For our light affliction, which is for the moment, worketh for us more and more exceedingly an eternal weight of glory; while we look not at the things which are seen, but at the things which are not seen: for the things which are seen are temporal; but the things which are not seen are eternal. For we know that if the earthly house of our tent be dissolved, *we have a building from God, a house not made with hands, eternal in the heavens*' (Rom. viii. 18; 2 Cor. iv. 16—v. 1).

III. THE STEM OF THE TREE

As the Apostle's olive tree grows upwards so, too, like any tree of the natural realm, its stem becomes progressively narrower. The first presage of this principle was given to Abraham after the birth of Ishmael and while Isaac, though promised, was as yet unborn. In response to the patriarch's petition, 'O that Ishmael might live before Thee!' God affirmed, 'My covenant will I establish with Isaac' (Gn. xvii. 18, 21). When in due course Isaac was born, the Almighty again asserted this purpose with great particularity: 'In Isaac shall thy seed be called' (Gn. xxi. 12). The trunk of the tree was narrowed yet further in connection with the offspring of Isaac: Jacob not only purchased his brother's birthright for a dish of broth, but also, though the younger son, obtained the paternal blessing which normally should have gone to Esau the firstborn (Gn. xxv. 29 ff., xxvii). In turn Jacob's prophetic benediction from his death-bed demarcated Judah from among all his sons as the one through whom in a special manner the line of the promise was to be continued (Gn. xlix. 8 ff.). Subsequently the blessing pronounced upon the descendants of Judah was confined more narrowly still in its outworkings to the family of David, in connection with whom it was promised that the Messianic King would be of his stock, and the glories of that kingdom eternal: 'Thine house and thy kingdom shall be made sure for ever before thee; thy throne shall be established for ever' (2 Sa. vii. 16, R.V.). This promise of an eternal kingdom in its essence necessarily looked forward to the unending reign of an Eternal King. 'The establishment of the kingdom and throne of David *for ever,* points incontrovertibly beyond the time of Solomon, and to the eternal continuance of a seed of David. . . . We must not reduce the idea of eternity to the popular notion of a long incalculable period, but must take it in an absolute sense, as the promise is evidently understood in Ps. lxxxix. 29: 'I set his seed for ever, and his throne as the days of heaven.' No earthly kingdom, and no posterity of any single man, has eternal duration. . . . The posterity of David, therefore, could only last for ever by running out in a person who lives for ever, *i.e.* by culminating in the Messiah, who lives for ever, and of whose kingdom there is no end' (Keil and Delitzsch, *comm. in loc.*).

That these remarkable promises of God to the saints of old actually had in view a single messianic Personage is further corroborated by St. Paul's interpretation of the Abrahamic covenant. It has already been shown how the New Testament leads us to understand that the gaze of Abraham was directed away from the perishable fabric of this world and fixed upon an abode of God's making which is 'eternal in the heavens.' But the inspired Apostle conducts us still deeper into the mysterious meaning of the divine covenant with Abraham, when he instructs us that the 'seed' of the patriarch to which the promise referred is to be interpreted specifically as pointing to none other than Christ Himself. That is, the stem of the olive tree reaches its narrowest, its consummating point, in the person of the Messiah. It was exactly this same truth which the devout Zacharias was enabled to grasp shortly before the birth of Mary's Son. He blessed Almighty God because of the crowning knowledge that, by the impending advent of the person of Jesus, He was about 'to perform the mercy promised to our fathers, and to remember His holy covenant: the oath which He sware to our father Abraham' (Lk. i. 72, 73).

St. Paul expounds this matter in the following way: 'Now to Abraham were the promises spoken, and to his seed. He saith not, And to seeds, as of many; but as of one, *And to thy seed, which is Christ'* (Gal. iii. 16, R.V.). Not that St. Paul is dependent for the validity of his interpretation upon a mere point of grammar: he appeals to the use of the singular noun simply as a confirmation of the truth of his exegesis. But, it may be objected, the singular noun 'seed' may be employed just as well in a collective as in an individualistic sense. To this one must interpose the rejoinder that St. Paul was not only well aware of this fact, but also in this very same passage adds an interpretation which is based upon the collective sense of the term. 'Ye are all one in Christ Jesus,' he assures his readers; 'and if ye are Christ's, *then are ye Abraham's seed,* and heirs according to the promise' (Gal. iii. 28, 29). Nor does this collective interpretation in any way contradict the individualistic interpretation, for, as is clearly indicated by the Apostle's argument here, Christian believers are only accounted as Abraham's seed on the ground of their being identified with Christ through faith; they (the collective 'seed') are seen and accepted *in Him* (the single 'seed'). And thus the term 'seed' is to be understood in both a collective and individualistic sense: the one is the complement, not the contradiction of the other. But the collectiveness may be understood ever and only in the all-enfolding unity of the Person of the Messiah: *all* are truly *one* 'in Christ Jesus.'

IV. THE BRANCHES OF THE TREE

Though the narrowest point in the stem of this tree of divine promise is reached in the Person of Christ, yet in no respect does this represent a narrowing in the beneficent purposes of God. In Christ, indeed, we find the true fulfilment of all God's promises: 'All the promises of God have their Yea in Him' (2 Cor. i. 20, *Corrected English New Testament*). And it is at this consummating or nuclear point, namely Christ, that the branches also have their union with the trunk of the tree.

The continuing fruitfulness and well-being of the several branches depends upon a vital union with the trunk whereby they are enabled to partake of 'the root and fatness of the tree' (Rom. xi. 17). Should this organic participation be interrupted in the case of any branch, with the inevitable result that it becomes a fruitless and moribund encumbrance, the divine Husbandman breaks it off, and in its stead grafts in a branch from a wild olive tree. It is plain from the context of this apostolic allegory that the 'natural' branches represent the Jews and the branches of the 'wild' olive tree represent the Gentiles, and that the vital principle of union between branch and stem, whether the branch be natural or engrafted, is that of *faith*. The natural branches were broken off '*because of unbelief*,' and the engrafted branches maintain their position of privilege '*by faith*.' Yet, if they do not continue in faith, the latter will also be cut off; and those natural branches that have been broken off, '*if they abide not still in unbelief*, shall be grafted in: for God is able to graft them in again' (Rom. xi. 20-23; cf. Je. xi. 16, 17).

The first thing that we learn from this Scripture is the fact of the unassailable sovereignty and supremacy of

Almighty God, a matter which St. Paul emphasizes with great insistence in dealing with this subject. The frailty and fickleness of man cannot in any way frustrate the progress and fulfilment of God's purposes: He both breaks off and grafts in, to the end that His husbandry is unimpaired in vigour and in fruitfulness. Whether by Jew or by Gentile, His perfect work is set forward. And we also learn that all the branches, both Jewish and Gentile, are supported by the same root and nourished by the same fatness or sap, and that for all alike the requirement for continuance in the organic communion of this state of blessing is simply and solely that of faith.

This is the kernel of the Apostle's argument in Romans ix-xi, which is the most important passage in the New Testament on the subject of the relationship between Jew and Gentile. 'I have great sorrow and unceasing pain in my heart,' he says; 'for I could wish that I myself were accursed from Christ for the sake of my brethren, my kinsmen according to the flesh: who are Israelites; to whom belong the adoption, and the glory, and the covenants, and the living of the law, and the service of God, and the promises; whose are the fathers, and from whom, as regards the flesh, is the Christ, who is over all, God blessed for ever' (Rom. ix. 2-5, *Corrected English New Testament*). We are not, however, to suppose (he continues) that through their lamentable defection the word of God has been frustrated and rendered ineffectual. This is never the case with any word of God, and such a supposition betrays a woeful misunderstanding of the inflexible nature of the divine purposes. It is not by any means being of the seed of Abraham according to the flesh that ensures acceptability with God; otherwise the lines of Ishmael and of Esau would also have been lines of blessing in the purpose of God. God had said to Abraham, 'In Isaac shall thy seed be called'— that is, in the son of promise, who was the fruit and crown of Abraham's great faith. This demonstrates in itself that 'it is not the children of the flesh that are children of God; but the children of the promise are reckoned as the seed'

(Rom. ix. 6-8). This, of course, coheres with the fundamental evangelical principle enunciated by our Lord: 'That which is born of the flesh is flesh, and that which is born of the Spirit is spirit: marvel not that I said unto thee, Ye must be born again' (Jn. iii. 6, 7).

The promise of God was coupled with the faith of Abraham, and it is ever faith that links human hearts to the blessings of the divine covenant and identifies them, whether Jew or Gentile, bond or free, male or female, with the true seed of Abraham. 'Ye are all the children of God by faith in Christ Jesus,' affirms the Apostle; 'and if ye are Christ's, then are ye Abraham's seed, and heirs according to the promise' (Gal. iii. 26-29).

In another place St. Paul insists upon this same basic truth with, if possible, even greater earnestness; it is, indeed, the *leit-motif* of all his doctrinal writings: 'The promise,' he asserts, 'that he should be the heir of the world, was not to Abraham, or to his seed, through the law, but through the righteousness of faith.' It was given to the patriarch, under the circumstances already described, by God, 'who quickeneth the dead, and calleth those things which be not as though they were.' The notable faith of Abraham is shown in that he, 'against all hope, yet in hope, believed to this end, that he might become the father of many nations; according to that which was spoken, So shall thy seed be; and not being weak in faith, he considered his own body—to all intents dead, for he was about a hundred years old—and the deadness of Sarah's womb, yet staggered not at the promise of God through unbelief; but waxed strong through faith, giving glory to God, and being fully persuaded that, what God had promised, He was able also to perform. And therefore his faith was reckoned to him for righteousness. Nor was it written for Abraham's sake alone, that righteousness was reckoned to him; but for our sake also, to whom it shall be reckoned, if we believe on Him that raised up Jesus our Lord from the dead' (Rom. iv. 13-24, *Corrected English New Testament*).

But let us clearly see that God does not demand from us

merely faith in connection with a mysterious promise of an ancient day, but a very definite faith in connection with the fulfilment and consummation of that very promise in the person of Jesus Christ. Abraham peered forward towards the distant fulfilment of the promise: we look back in the fuller light of the New Testament upon its consummation, and are without excuse if our understanding of its content is not in proportion more complete than that of the patriarch. Yet, even so, the faith and spiritual perception of Abraham were so remarkable that he actually anticipated and, by the appropriation of a clear hope, rejoiced in the day of Christ: 'Your father Abraham rejoiced to see My day; and he saw it, and was glad,' our Lord assured the Jews who were seeking to controvert His teaching (Jn. viii. 56).

Now, the apprehension of this important truth directs us to a correct understanding of the inner meaning of God's promise to Abraham that he would become the father of many nations. Externally, of course, we have seen that this is referable to the vast numbers of his earthly descendents. But the deeper interpretation of this promise leads us to perceive that in their spiritual and ultimate significance the purposes of God were of a far different kind. The patriarch, says Calvin, 'was not called the father of many nations, because his seed was to be divided into many nations; but rather, because many nations were to be gathered together unto him' (*Comm. in* Gn. xvii. 6). God had in view not only the spreading out of the natural branches of the tree, but also, and even particularly, the grafting in of other branches from the wild olive tree, on the grounds of their faith. That this is so is explicitly borne out by St. Paul when he plainly states that 'the Scripture, *foreseeing that God would justify the Gentiles by faith,* preached the gospel beforehand unto Abraham, saying, In thee shall all the nations be blessed' (Gal. iii. 8, R.V.). Thus the engrafting of the Gentiles was by no means a new purpose of God, but an age-old one implied even in the terms of His covenant with Abraham.

God's design for universal blessing is apparent in every section of the Old Testament, and the Jew with his wide knowledge of the Scriptures should have been on his guard against the spirit of pharisaic exclusivism which was so prevalent in the apostolic times. St. Paul reminds his readers in Rome of the word of God spoken through Moses, whereby God's total independence is asserted: 'I will have mercy on whom I will have mercy, and I will have compassion on whom I will have compassion.' He reminds them of the words spoken through the prophet Hosea which struck at the Jewish national pride: 'I will call them My people, who were not My people, and her beloved, who was not beloved. And, in the place where it was said to them, Ye are not My people, there shall they be called the children of the living God.' He reminds them of the boldness of Isaiah in saying concerning the Gentiles: 'I was found by them that sought Me not; I was made manifest unto them that asked not after Me'; whereas in this same place it is said concerning Israel: 'All day long I stretched forth My hands to a disobedient and gainsaying people.' Even Moses had prophesied: 'I will move you to jealousy by those who are no people, and by a nation void of understanding I will provoke you.' Moreover, the universal scope of God's grace was proclaimed through Isaiah: 'Whosoever believeth on Him shall not be put to shame,' and Joel had announced: 'Whosoever shall call upon the Name of the Lord shall be saved.' Therefore, the Apostle concludes, 'there is no distinction between Jew and Greek, seeing that the same Lord is Lord over all, and is rich unto all that call upon Him' (Rom. ix. 15, 25, 26, x. 20, 21, 19, 11, 13, 12. Cf. Rom. xv. 9-12 for further citations adduced by St. Paul from the Old Testament).

Part and parcel with all this is St. Paul's reminder of the Old Testament doctrine that only a *remnant* of Israel would be saved, not the whole people without discrimination. This, too, was a blow at the national pride of the Jews. The Apostle quotes the words of the prophet Isaiah: 'Though the number of the children of Israel be as the sand of the sea, a remnant shall be saved'; and, 'Except the Lord of Sabaoth had left us a seed, we had been as Sodom, and had been made like unto Gomorrah.' Again, he points out that by no means all who of old heard the good news in Israel paid heed to it; even as the same prophet complains: 'Lord, who hath believed our report?' In the days of the prophet Elijah, when godlessness and apostasy flourished on all sides, God had preserved a remnant who had not bowed the knee to Baal; and the Apostle declares that the same was true of his own day: 'Even so then at this present time also there is a remnant according to the election of grace' (Rom. ix. 27-29, x. 16, xi. 3-5).

St. Paul himself and the other Apostles were members of this remnant according to the election of grace in the midst of an unresponsive people. We see this principle of the unbelieving majority as opposed to the faithful remnant, and of the divine purpose of blessing to the Gentiles, at work in Pisidian Antioch, where the Jews met the message of the gospel with cold hostility and refused to heed the solemn warnings of Holy Scripture. After proclaiming the good news of Jesus Christ, Paul and Barnabas uttered this earnest admonition: 'Beware therefore, lest that come upon you, which is spoken in the prophets, Behold, ye despisers, and wonder, and perish, for I work a work in your days, a work which ye will in no wise believe, though a man declare it to you.' The Jews, however, were filled with jealousy, and contradicted the things which were spoken by Paul, and blasphemed. Then the Apostles spoke out boldly, and declared their intention of obeying the scriptural commission by taking the gospel to the Gentiles, whom these Jews, blinded by pride, considered to be beyond the scope of God's grace. 'It was necessary,' said Paul and Barnabas, 'that the word of God should first be spoken to you. Seeing that ye thrust it from you, and judge yourselves unworthy of eternal life, lo, we turn to the Gentiles. For so hath the Lord commanded us, saying, I have set thee for a light to the Gentiles, that thou shouldest be for salvation unto the uttermost parts of the earth' (Acts xiii.

38-48). And so through their fall salvation came to the Gentiles, and the whole world was enriched; branches from the wild olive tree were grafted in to replace the natural branches which were broken off because of unbelief (Rom. xi. 11, 12, 17 ff.).

We are now in a position to understand clearly St. Paul's dictum: 'They are not all Israel, which are of Israel' (Rom. ix. 6). Those who are of the stock of Israel according to the flesh, although thereby placed in a position of privilege, are not in virtue of this standing automatically constituted members of the true or spiritual Israel: 'It is not the children of the flesh that are children of God' (Rom. ix. 8, R.V.). It is faith that justifies, and grace that elects; and God's blessing is designed for all the nations of the earth. Thus the full company of the redeemed in glory, as seen by St. John, is 'a great multitude, which no man could number, of all nations, and kindreds, and people, and tongues,' their robes washed and made white in the blood of the Lamb (Rev. vii. 9, 14). The author of that great eleventh chapter of Hebrews, which describes how the perspective of the patriarchs penetrated right into heaven itself, tells us that as the reward of faith 'therefore sprang there even of one, and him as good as dead, so many as the stars of the sky in multitude, and as the sand which is by the sea shore innumerable' (Heb. xi. 12); and in the innumerable multitude of the redeemed in heaven, drawn from every clime and race, we see the glorious ultimate fulfilment of God's ancient promise to Abraham, that He would multiply his seed as the stars of heaven, and as the sand which is upon the sea shore, and that in his seed should all the nations of the earth be blessed (Gn. xxii. 17, 18).

The truth against which the Jew hardened his heart, and which he persistently refused to learn, was that 'there is no respect of persons with God' (Rom. ii. 11), and that the universal grace of God is in fact founded upon the universal sinfulness and need of mankind, a point which St. Paul, supported by the unequivocal statements of Scripture, hammers home in the third chapter of his Epistle to the

Romans. All, both Jews and Greeks, are under sin; there is none righteous, no, not one; there is no distinction, for all have sinned and come short of the glory of God; God is the God, not only of the Jews, but of the Gentiles also; He justifies both the circumcision and also the uncircumcision through faith.

Circumcision, indeed, the distinctive mark of the Israelite, was not instituted by God as a sign of superiority, but as a seal and token of the acceptance with God which comes through faith in His word, and was intended as a constant reminder to the human heart of the need for the renunciation of all fleshly vanity and for the exercise of true humility and dependence towards God. Abraham himself, the honoured patriarch of the Israelites, was accounted righteous through his faith, without regard to the fact that he was at the time uncircumcised, a significant consideration, as the Apostle reminded his Jewish readers: 'He receiveth the sign of circumcision, a seal of the righteousness of the faith which he had while he was still in uncircumcision; that he might be the father of all them that believe, though they be in uncircumcision, that righteousness might be reckoned unto them also; and that he might be the father of circumcision to them who not only are of the circumcision, but who also walk in the steps of that faith of our father Abraham which he had in uncircumcision' (Rom. iv. 11, 12).

That this is the true significance of the rite of circumcision is made perfectly plain in the pages of the Old Testament itself, so that there was no reason for the devout Jew to be in error concerning its real import, or to imagine that it was a mere fleshly formality intended to foster his national pride. (In any case, there were other peoples in the ancient world besides the Israelites who practised the custom of circumcision.) Thus the Levitical writing alludes to their 'uncircumcised hearts' (Lv. xxvi. 41); and Moses enjoined his wayward people in these terms: 'Circumcise therefore the foreskin of your heart, and be no more stiffnecked' (Dt. x. 16). This great leader of old also told the

Israelites: 'The Lord thy God will circumcise thine heart, and the heart of thy seed, to love the Lord thy God with all thine heart and with all thy soul, that thou mayest live' (Dt. xxx. 6). And in a subsequent day of national crisis the prophet Jeremiah offered this warning to the people of Judah: 'Thus saith the Lord to the men of Judah and Jerusalem. . . . Circumcise yourselves to the Lord, and take away the foreskins of your heart, ye men of Judah and inhabitants of Jerusalem; lest My fury come forth like fire, and burn that none can quench it, because of the evil of your doings' (Je. iv. 3, 4).

St. Paul, in speaking to the Jew, insists upon this same inner emphasis: 'He is not a Jew, which is one outwardly; neither is that circumcision, which is outward in the flesh: but he is a Jew, which is one inwardly; and circumcision is that of the heart, in the spirit, and not in the letter; whose praise is not of men, but of God' (Rom. ii. 28, 29). And, in speaking to the Christian, the Apostle says that in Christ he is 'circumcised with a circumcision not made with hands, in the putting off of the body of the flesh, in the circumcision of Christ' (Col. ii. 11. R.V.). Again, he reminds us that, as those who are saved by faith in the Lord Jesus Christ, 'we are the circumcision, who worship by the Spirit of God, and glory in Christ Jesus, and have no confidence in the flesh' (Phil. iii. 3. R.V.).

All outward ceremonial, though it be divinely instituted, is nothing and valueless, unless it be accompanied with a sincere corresponding attitude of heart in repentance and trust; thus alone may it become the vehicle of a vital religion. That is the great lesson which the Apostle has to teach, and that is the lesson which the Jews were so unwilling to learn. The Jews enjoyed a unique and special advantage, chiefly in that the oracles of God had been committed to them (Rom. iii. 2; cf. ix. 4); and yet through the wanton hardness of their hearts they misinterpreted their trust in a carnal and arrogant manner, and destroyed their privilege, bartering it like profane Esau for one morsel of meat, that of confidence in the flesh. They did not relish being reminded that God is not by any means limited in manifestation or in blessing to one 'promised land' or to one 'chosen people,' or that the river of His grace which flows from the sanctuary was never intended to be dammed up, but rather, growing ever deeper and broader, was designed from the very beginning to bring life and refreshment even into the thirsty desert of the heathen world (Ezk. xlvii). They did not wish to see branches from the wild olive tree grafted into the trunk of the natural tree and sharing in the rich blessings of its root and fatness. Least of all in their blind pride did they imagine that it could ever be possible for them to be cut off from their position of privilege because of unbelief.

To such, who boasted, 'We be Abraham's seed, and were never in bondage to any man,' our Lord replied with these incriminating words: 'If ye were Abraham's children, ye would do the works of Abraham. . . . Ye are of your father the devil, and the lusts of your father ye will do' (Jn. viii. 33, 39, 44).

To such the first Christian martyr, in an oration of pointed brilliance (Acts vii), showed by unmistakable implication that the presence of Jehovah, even in the case of their venerable forebears, was not confined to the land of Canaan—indeed, that the lives of the patriarchs, as they were directed and controlled by God, were more intimately connected with the countries of the heathen than with the land of promise. The implications of this inspired address before the Sanhedrin were too plain to be missed, and cut the hearers to the heart. Your great forefather Abraham (said Stephen to them in effect), of whose stock you boast yourselves to be, was actually a foreigner, a Chaldean by birth. God manifested Himself to him in Mesopotamia, *not* in Judaea. Indeed, in the latter land the patriarch had not even a foot's breadth of soil to call his own, with the exception of a place of *burial* which he had had to purchase from the inhabitants for a sum of money. Even this sepulchre which he bought was in a spot despised by you—Shechem, a city of the Samaritans, with whom you have no dealings. He entered the land as an uncircumcised man; nor was there any temple there in his day. Your honoured ancestors wickedly sold Joseph into Egypt; but God was with him in that foreign country, and exalted him there. It was to Egypt, *not* Judaea—in fact, *from* Judaea—that the insignificant handful of your forefathers had to flee as suppliants, in order that their family might survive and not be wiped off the face of the earth by famine. Again, it was in Egypt that they became a great and numerous people. Your great lawgiver Moses was born in Egypt; he was nurtured and educated in the palace of Pharaoh, and became learned in Egyptian wisdom. Remember, too, that your forebears rejected Moses as their leader and deliverer, when he wished to help them, and caused him to flee and become a sojourner in the strange land of Midian for a third part of his lifetime. Yet God appeared to him in the wilderness, and proclaimed the locality of His manifestation, though foreign soil, to be holy ground. The holy law and oracles of God were entrusted to Moses at Mount Sinai in Arabia, *not* in the promised land; and for forty years he led the Israelites through the wilderness, but he himself never set foot on the soil of Judaea. God showed His wonders and signs to them in Egypt, at the Red Sea, and in the wilderness, heathen territory, all of it; yet your ancestors, whose memory you so proudly cherish, were disobedient, rebellious, idolatrous, and unmindful of all God's goodness to them. Even the divinely ordained tabernacle was a wilderness institution; and some hundreds of years later, in the days of king David, there was still no temple in the city of David, though he found favour with God, and earnestly desired to build Him a house. This privilege was granted to Solomon, the king who, none the less, was guilty of setting the nation off on the disastrous decline towards the apostasy and false worship which ended in the shame of the Assyrian and Babylonian captivities.

Just as their forefathers, moved with envy, had sold Joseph into bondage, had rejected Moses as their deliverer, and had persecuted and put to death God's messengers the prophets, who had foretold the coming of the Just One, so, too, these religious leaders before whom Stephen was arraigned had blindly resisted the Holy Ghost, misinterpreted the Holy Scriptures, and spurned the Holy Son of God. And in doing so they were not only destroying their own souls, but those too of the people who looked to them for spiritual guidance. This is the great tragedy of the Jewish people. It is this attitude of unbelief that has caused the natural branches to be cut off and left to endure centuries of languishing grief and suffering. But God is still merciful and gracious: He whom they rejected still offers Himself as their mighty Deliverer and Messiah. 'They also, *if they abide not still in unbelief,* shall be grafted in: for God is able to graft them in again.'

That is a day to be prayed for: the day of the restoration of the natural branches of the olive tree; which would mean a day of perhaps unprecedented blessing to the world through them. 'If their fall is the enriching of the world, and their loss the enriching of the Gentiles; how much more their fulness?' (Rom. xi. 12, *Corrected English New Testament.*) Meanwhile there is no room for pride or smugness on the part of the Gentiles; indeed, in the appalling spiritual condition of our world today there is a grave danger lest the severity of God should descend upon those nations which are failing to continue in His goodness, and lest the engrafted branches should be cut off also (Rom. xi. 19-22). The fate of Germany is a dreadful warning at the present time to other privileged nations—the British nation not least—of the disaster, material and moral as well as spiritual, which follows inevitably upon arrogance and glorying in the flesh and defection from the true faith as it is in Christ Jesus. It is time for the so-called 'Christian' nations to heed this warning, and to cease putting their confidence in merely human counsel and in the possession of atomic secrets. What is essential and of prime importance is to return to God in humility and contrition and in acknowledgment of His supreme sovereignty and our utter dependence. It is, as ever, unbelief that severs a people from the grace and favour of God, and causes it to wither and rot.

What may be said concerning the future? St. Paul, no doubt necessarily, is somewhat obscure in treating of 'this mystery,' and I certainly do not wish to dogmatize in connection with matters that are but indistinctly revealed. It would seem, however, that the fulness of Israel will be preceded by the fulness of the Gentiles. By the former the Apostle probably wishes to signify the completion of the number of the elect from among the nation of Israel through the acknowledgment of Jesus as their Messiah and Deliverer, who will remove ungodliness from Jacob and take away their sins (Rom. xi. 25-27). The fulness of the Gentiles implies the fulfilment of our Lord's final commission to His followers to go into all the world and preach the gospel to every creature, and to be His witnesses to the uttermost parts of the earth (Mk. xvi. 15; Acts i. 8). Then truly people from every quarter of the globe will be able to confess before their Lord: 'Thou wast slain, and hast redeemed us to God by thy blood out of every kindred and tongue and people and nation' (Rev. v. 9). Up till now the conversion of Jews has only been, as it were, occasional and incidental. St. Paul refers to this fact when he says that 'a partial hardening hath befallen Israel, until the fulness of the Gentiles shall have come in.' If, then, we wish to see the fulness of Israel, which will mean an influx into our world of revitalizing spiritual power (Rom. xi. 16), we must do our utmost to hasten the fulness of the Gentiles, that is to say, we must promote with the greatest possible vigour and zeal the missionary task of evangelizing the heathen in every corner of the earth. The faithful performance of this world-wide task will help to bring enlightenment to the heart of the Jewish people and to convince them that He who is rich in mercy to every Gentile believer is waiting to bestow the treasures of His grace upon them also.

Until this task is done, the family circle will not be completed, the elder brother, who because of his anger has remained outside, will not be brought in to share in the festal joys of the redeemed. And so the challenge comes to us in these last days to evangelize tirelessly and with thoroughness, so that the fulness of both Jews and Gentiles may be achieved. 'Thus all Israel shall be saved' (Rom. xi. 26), both Jew and Gentile, the true and eternal seed of Abraham by faith in the Name of the Lord Jesus Christ, 'the Israel of God' (Gal. vi. 16); and the number of the elect shall have been filled up according to the perfect purposes of Almighty God.

Finally, let us acknowledge the immutability of the divine purposes: the promise of unspeakable blessing to all the nations of the earth through Abraham and his seed, pre-eminently and perfectly fulfilled in and through the glorious Person of Jesus Christ, by identification with whom all His saints are made one; and the defection of the Jews, although constituting them enemies to the gospel, yet by no means cancelling the election of the Jews, who are beloved for the fathers' sake. 'For the gifts and calling of God are never regretted by God.' For as the Gentiles in time past were disobedient to God, but have now obtained mercy by the disobedience of the Jews, even so have the Jews also now been disobedient, that by the mercy shown to the Gentiles they too may obtain mercy. 'For God hath shut up all under disobedience, that He might have mercy upon all,' both Gentile and Jew (Rom. xi. 28-32, R.V.).

Let us acknowledge, too, the inscrutability of the divine purposes: for here we find the Jew, who was at the first favoured with such unique promises and privileges, being the last to enter upon the enjoyment of the universal blessing of the gospel, and that, too, by the instrumentality of the Gentiles; he is now in fact an Ishmael, cast out and blindly perishing in the wilderness, until his eyes are opened by God to see, even at his side and within his reach, the well of the life-giving water of the gospel. So we observe the truth of the Scripture which informs us that 'the last shall be first, and the first last' (Mt. xx. 16).

'O the depth of the riches both of the wisdom and knowledge of God! How unsearchable are His judgments, and

His ways past finding out! For who hath known the mind of the Lord? Or who hath been His counsellor? Or who hath first given to Him, and it shall be recompensed unto him again? For of Him, and through Him, and to Him, are all things: To whom be glory for ever and ever. Amen' (Rom. xi. 33-36).

www.ingramcontent.com/pod-product-compliance
Lightning Source LLC
LaVergne TN
LVHW010549100826
845148LV00013B/2671